little backyard animals

Coyotes

John Willis

LET'S READ
AV²
BY WEIGL™
ADDED VALUE • AUDIO VISUAL

AV² provides enriched content that supplements and complements this book. Weigl's AV² books strive to create inspired learning and engage young minds in a total learning experience.

Your AV² Media Enhanced books come alive with...

Go to **www.av2books.com**, and enter this book's unique code.

BOOK CODE

F273233

AV² by Weigl brings you media enhanced books that support active learning.

Audio
Listen to sections of the book read aloud.

Video
Watch informative video clips.

Embedded Weblinks
Gain additional information for research.

Try This!
Complete activities and hands-on experiments.

Key Words
Study vocabulary, and complete a matching word activity.

Quizzes
Test your knowledge.

Slide Show
View images and captions, and prepare a presentation.

... and much, much more!

Published by AV² by Weigl
350 5th Avenue, 59th Floor New York, NY 10118
Website: www.av2books.com

Library of Congress Control Number: 2015958826

ISBN 978-1-4896-4745-0 (hardcover)
ISBN 978-1-4896-4809-9 (softcover)
ISBN 978-1-4896-4746-7 (multi-user eBook)

Printed in the United States of America in Brainerd, Minnesota
1 2 3 4 5 6 7 8 9 0 19 18 17 16 15

122015
041215

Project Coordinator: Heather Kissock
Designer: Terry Paulhus

Coyotes

In this book, I will tell you about their

home

food

family

and

how they grow up.

One day, I was riding my bike down the back lane. I saw two big, brown dogs digging a hole on the side of the hill behind my house.

I went back home and told my mom. She said they could have been coyotes.

My mom said that coyotes dig holes
when they are about to have babies.
She said the hole leads to the den.
The mother and father coyotes
raise their pups there.

My mom said that I should keep away
from the den to stay safe. She told me
that I could watch the coyotes
with my binoculars.

I watched for the coyotes every day.
One coyote stayed close to the den.
I could sometimes see it digging.

The other coyote would leave the
den and then come back. It often
brought food to the den.

My mom said that the coyote staying close to the den was the mother. The other coyote was the father.

After a couple of weeks, I could no longer see the mother coyote. My mom said that she was now living in the den. She was about to have her babies.

I could not wait to see the babies. My mom said they would not come out of the den right away. Their mother would keep them inside for another two weeks.

She said the pups were too tiny when first born. They needed their mother's milk to help them grow.

It was a long wait, but one day I finally saw the coyote pups outside of the den. They were rolling in the grass and playing.

Their eyes were open, and their ears were perky. They still lived in the den most of the time.

Summer came, and I saw the pups leave the den with their parents. They came back later in the day. My mom told me that the parents were teaching their pups how to find food.

A few days later, I saw one of the pups chase after a squirrel.

Almost six months passed. The young coyotes started to go hunting for food on their own.

My mom said that they would soon be ready to leave home and live on their own.

It was starting to get colder. I did not see the coyotes as much anymore. Some of them had gone to live on their own.

My mom told me that the rest of the family would stay together for the winter.

The next spring, I decided to look at the den again with my binoculars.

A new family of coyotes was now living there.

KEY WORDS

Research has shown that as much as 65 percent of all written material published in English is made up of 300 words. These 300 words cannot be taught using pictures or learned by sounding them out. They must be recognized by sight. This book contains 102 common sight words to help young readers improve their reading fluency and comprehension. This book also teaches young readers several important content words, such as proper nouns. These words are paired with pictures to aid in learning and improve understanding.

Page	Sight Words First Appearance
4	a, and, back, been, big, could, day, down, have, home, house, I, my, of, on, one, said, saw, she, side, the, they, two, was, went
7	about, are, away, father, from, keep, me, mother, should, that, their, there, to, watch, when, with
9	close, come, every, food, for, it, leave, often, other, see, sometimes, then, would
10	after, her, in, no, now
13	another, first, grow, help, not, out, right, them, too, were
15	but, eyes, lived, long, most, open, still, time
16	came, few, find, how, later
19	almost, be, go, own, soon, started, young
20	as, did, family, get, had, much, some, together
22	again, at, look, next
23	new

Page	Content Words First Appearance
4	bike, coyotes, dogs, hill, hole, lane, mom
7	babies, binoculars, den, pups
10	weeks
13	milk
15	ears, grass
16	parents, squirrel, summer
19	months
20	winter
22	spring

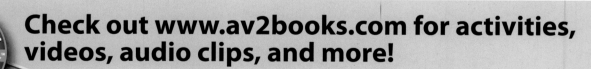